First World War
and Army of Occupation
War Diary
France, Belgium and Germany

59 DIVISION
178 Infantry Brigade
Headquarters
28 February 1915 - 31 May 1916

WO95/3024/1

The Naval & Military Press Ltd
www.nmarchive.com
Published in association with The National Archives

Published by

The Naval & Military Press Ltd

Unit 10 Ridgewood Industrial Park,

Uckfield, East Sussex,

TN22 5QE England

Tel: +44 (0) 1825 749494

www.naval-military-press.com

www.nmarchive.com

This diary has been reprinted in facsimile from the original. Any imperfections are inevitably reproduced and the quality may fall short of modern type and cartographic standards.

© **Crown Copyright**
Images reproduced by permission of The National Archives, London, England, 2015.

Contents

Document type	Place/Title	Date From	Date To
Heading	178 Inf Brigade 2/1 Notts & Derby Feb 1915 May 1916		
Heading	59 Division (Formerly 2nd North Midland Div) 178 Inf Brigade (2/1 Notts & Derby) 1915 Feb-1916 May		
Heading	War Diary of 2/1 Sherwood Forester Inf Bde From 1st To 28 February 1915 Volume I		
War Diary	Luton, 1915	23/02/1915	28/02/1915
Miscellaneous	Statement to Accompany War Diary for February 1915		
Heading	War Diary of 2/1 Sherwood Forester Inf Bde From 1st To 31 March 1915 Volume II		
War Diary	Luton	04/03/1915	20/03/1915
Miscellaneous	Statement to Accompany War Diary		
Heading	War Diary of Headquarter 2/1 Sherwood Infantry Brigade From 1-30 April 1915 Volume III		
War Diary	Luton	16/04/1915	18/04/1915
Miscellaneous	Statement to Accompany War Diary for April 1915		
Heading	War Diary & Statement Of Headquarters 2/1 Notts & Durby Inf Bde From 1st To 31st May 1915 Volume IV		
War Diary	Luton	07/05/1915	07/05/1915
Miscellaneous	Statement to Accompany War Diary for May 1915		
Heading	War Diary & Statement Of Headquarters 2/1 Notts Durby Inf Bde From 1st To 30 June 1915 Volume V		
War Diary	Luton	04/06/1915	04/06/1915
War Diary	Dunstable	07/06/1915	27/06/1915
Miscellaneous	Statement to Accompany War Diary for June 1915		
Heading	War Diary & Statement Of Headquarters 2/1 Sher for Inf Bde From 1st To 31 July 1915 Vol VI		
War Diary	Dunstable	12/07/1915	23/07/1915
Miscellaneous	Statement to Accompany War Diary for July 1915		
Heading	War Diary & Statement Of Headquarters 178 Infantry Brigade From 1st To 31st August 1915 Volume VII		
War Diary	Dunstable	01/08/1915	11/08/1915
War Diary	Watford Herts	15/08/1915	15/08/1915
Miscellaneous	Statement to Accompany War Diary for August 1918		
Heading	War Diary of Headquarters 178 Infantry Brigade From 1st To 30th September 1915 Volume VIII		
War Diary	Watford	30/09/1915	30/09/1915
Miscellaneous	Statement to Accompany War Diary September 1915		
Heading	War Diary & Statement Of Headquarters 178 Infantry Brigade From 1st To 31st October 1915 Volume IX		
War Diary	Watford Cassiobury Park Camp	01/10/1915	13/10/1915
War Diary	Watford Town	18/10/1915	19/10/1915
Miscellaneous	Statement to Accompany War Diary for October 1915		
Miscellaneous	Orders Issued To Troops Under My Command During The Camping Season		
Miscellaneous	A Resume of Orders Issued to Troops Under My Command, Whilst in Billets		
Heading	War Diary & Statement Of Headquarters 178 Inf Bde From 1st To 30 November 1915 Volume X		
War Diary	Watford	01/11/1915	30/11/1915

Miscellaneous	178th. Infantry Brigade Statement To Accompany War Diary For November 1915		
Heading	War Diary & Statement Of Headquarters 178 Inf Bde From 1st To 31 December 1915 Vl XI		
War Diary	Watford	01/12/1915	31/12/1915
Miscellaneous	Statement to Accompany War Diary for December 1915		
Heading	War Diary of Headquarters 178th Infantry Brigade From 1st To 31st January 1916 Volume XII		
War Diary	Watford	09/01/1916	29/01/1916
Miscellaneous	Statement to Accompany War Diary for January 1916		
Heading	War Diary of Headquarters 178 Infantry Bde From 1st To 29th February 1916 Vol XIII		
War Diary	Watford	03/02/1916	29/02/1916
Miscellaneous	Statement to Accompany War Diary for the Month of February 1916		
Heading	War Diary of Headquarters 178 Infantry Brigade From 1st To 31st March 1916 Volume XIV		
War Diary	Watford	04/03/1916	31/03/1916
Miscellaneous	Statement to Accompany War Diary for March 1916		
War Diary	Royal Hospital Kilmainham	01/05/1916	02/05/1916
War Diary	Royal Hospital Kilmainham Dublin	03/05/1916	31/05/1916

178 INF. BRIGADE

2/1 Notts Derby

FEB 1915 — MAY 1916

59 DIVISION
(formerly 2nd NORTH MIDLAND DIV)

178 INF BRIGADE
(2/1 Notts & Derby)

1915 FEB — 1916 MAY

59 DIV

178 BDE

Confidential

WAR DIARY

of

2/1 Sherwood Foresters. Inf: Bde

from 1st to 28th February 1915

Volume I

CONFIDENTIAL.

Headquarters,
2/1st Notts & Derby Infantry Brigade.

Army Form C. 2118.

Instructions regarding War Diaries and Intelligence Summaries are contained in F. S. Regs, Part II. and the Staff Manual respectively. Title pages will be prepared in manuscript.

WAR DIARY
or
INTELLIGENCE SUMMARY.
(Erase heading not required.)

Hour, Date, Place	Summary of Events and Information	Remarks and references to Appendices
LUTON, 1915.		
28th.February, 1915.	The Brigade concentrated at Luton, its War station, as follows:-	
	2/5th Bn.Sherwood Foresters. 17 Officers. 763 other ranks on the 3rd inst.	
	2/6th Bn. ditto 22 Officers. 892 other ranks -do-	
	2/7th Bn. ditto 18 Officers. 963 other ranks on the 1st inst.	
	2/8th Bn. ditto 21 Officers. 786 other ranks -do-	
	The Brigade moved into Essex by train to their respective stations for work on the permanent defences of London and instruction in entrenching, rivetting &c as follows:-	
	Brigade Hdqrs. 2 Officers. " 3 O.R. to Brentwood.	
	2/5th Bn.S.F. 14 " 783 " BROXBOURNE on the 8th inst.	Ap
	2/6th Bn.S.F. 21 " 912 " EPPING. on the 8th inst.	Ap
	2/7th Bn.S.F. 12 " 969 " ONGAR. ditto	
	2/8th Bn.S.F. 20 " 771 " BILLERICAY ditto	Ap

CONFIDENTIAL.

Army Form C. 2118.

Instructions regarding War Diaries and Intelligence Summaries are contained in F.S. Regs., Part II. and the Staff Manual respectively. Title pages will be prepared in manuscript.

WAR DIARY
or
INTELLIGENCE SUMMARY.
(Erase heading not required.)

Headquarters.
2/1st Notts & Derby Infantry Brigade.

Hour, Date, Place	Summary of Events and Information	Remarks and references to Appendices
	The field work was under the general direction of the C.R.E. N.L. Defences - Colonel F.E.F.Skey. R.E.	
	1 Officer and 10 Other ranks per Battalion proceeded to 1st Line units to take over all civilian transport and all documents left by them on proceeding overseas.	
	Civilian Transport Vehicles arrived at their respective Battalion Stations on or about the 18 - 20 February.	
	The Brigade moved back to Luton on the 24th February - Brigade Headquarters. 2 Officers. 3 Other ranks.	
	2/5th Bn. S.F. 25 " 1028 "	
	2/6th Bn. S.F. 22 " 964 "	
	2/7th Bn. S.F. 21 " 1099 "	
	2/8th Bn. S.F. 28 " 1038 "	
	The increase in strength arises owing to men of the Provisional Battalion (comprised of all units and already stationed in the Essex area) having been drafted into their respective 2nd Line Battalions before the Brigade returned to Luton.	

(9 29 6) W 8832–1107 100,000 10/13 H W V Forms/C. 2118/10.

CONFIDENTIAL.

Army Form C. 2118.

WAR DIARY Headquarters. 2/1st Notts & Derby Infantry Brigade.
or
INTELLIGENCE SUMMARY.

(*Erase heading not required.*)

Instructions regarding War Diaries and Intelligence Summaries are contained in F. S. Regs., Part II. and the Staff Manual respectively. Title pages will be prepared in manuscript.

Hour, Date, Place	Summary of Events and Information	Remarks and references to Appendices
	Japanese Rifles were issued to all Battalions at the end of the month.	
	All .303 Rifles except 200 per Battalion were returned to Weedon.	
	[signatures]	

Confidential

HEADQUARTERS.
2/1st NOTTS & DERBY INFANTRY BRIGADE.

STATEMENT TO ACCOMPANY WAR DIARY
for February 1915.

TRAINING.   The chief item of training for the month was digging and revetting. This was carried out by the whole Brigade in Essex and on the conclusion of the period the C.R.E. North London Defences expressed his great appreciation of the manner in which it had been carried out by all ranks. Stretcher bearers were detailed for training under a Medical Officer.

DISCIPLINE.   During the period while digging was in progress the discipline remained good.

ADMINISTRATIVE.   <u>Transport.</u> In the absence of Army pattern Transport little or no training could be done. Horses were issued to the Brigade towards the latter end of the month and considerable difficulty was experienced in the handling of them, there being very few men with any knowledge of horses and their management.

                  <u>Ordnance.</u> As most of the equipment &c. which came to the Brigade was a first issue, the County Associations provided nearly everything.

                  The 1914 Leather Equipment was very poor, the packs came away from the leather braces and all this equipment of the 2/5th and 2/6th Battalions had to be sent back to the makers to have the pack straps put higher on the packs and to be fastened with rivets in addition to the stitching.

BILLETING.   More stringent rules for billeting have now been instituted with regard to cubic air space and it is hoped that better general health will result.

                                                          Arthur N. Lee Capt
                                                          Brigade Major for C in Chief.

Confidential

WAR DIARY

of

2/1 Sherwood Foresters Inf: Bde

from 1st to 31st March 1915

Volume II

CONFIDENTIAL.   Army Form C. 2118.

Instructions regarding War Diaries and Intelligence
Summaries are contained in F.S. Regs., Part II.
and the Staff Manual respectively. Title pages
will be prepared in manuscript.

WAR DIARY
or
INTELLIGENCE SUMMARY.

(*Erase heading not required.*)

2/1 SHERWOOD FORESTER INFANTRY BRIGADE.

Hour, Date, Place	Summary of Events and Information	Remarks and references to Appendices
LUTON.		
March 1915.		
4	A Japanese Rifle Course (25 rounds per man) was started.	ap
10 "	A Musketry Officer Lieut E.W.Tidy (Corps of the School of Musketry) reported for duty as Brigade Musketry Officer.	ap
12 "	The 1st Foreign Draft Companies (200 men) of each Battalion started a .303 course.	ap
15 "	.303 course discontinued for lack of ammunition.	ap
20 "	1st Reinforcements (Base Details left by 1st. Line) started .303 course. This Brigade furnishing all Range duties, Officers and Instructors.	ap
"	11 Officers joined from 3rd. Line or on first commission.	ap
"	1 Officer sent for service overseas.	ap

Wrigley Bewres Co:
Cmdg. 2/1 Sher: In: Inf Bde

CONFIDENTIAL.   2/1 SHERWOOD FORESTER INFANTRY
                                              BRIGADE.

STATEMENT to accompany War Diary
for March 1915.

TRAINING.   General Training consisting chiefly of Physical Training, Platoon and Company Drill, Musketry elementary training and tests with some Battalion training and one Brigade Route march each week was carried out satisfactorily. The lack of good Instructors and competent N.C.O's is much felt and it is thought that on the formation of new Units in the future a proportion of such men should be retained from Units more advanced in training for the general benefit of such new Units (e.g. from the 1st. Line or from Regular Battalions). N.C.O's seem to have been chosen too early and without a proper examination of their capabilities in all Units.

DISCIPLINE. Considering the inexperience of Officers, the lack of knowledge in N.C.O's and the fact that the great majority of men in the Brigade were away from home and trade discipline for the first time in their lives, the men behave well and the discipline is good but there is much room for improvement.
The presence of so many medically unfit men in all Units is a great disadvantage. Men should not in my opinion be <u>enlisted</u> for Home Service during War time.

ADMINISTRATIVE SERVICES.

MEDICAL.   The general health of the Brigade is good. Inoculation against enteric is being pushed forward with all speed and there is only a small percentage of objectors.
The fact that the first Medical examination of recruits has been carelessly carried out shows itself very clearly

and in one Battalion there are as many as 70 men who are unfit for any kind of duty. Part of these men have been rejected on the departure of the 1st Line overseas but the majority were wrongly passed by civilian Doctors in the recruiting areas.

SUPPLY. Supply services are as good as can be expected.

TRANSPORT. Horses continue to be issued very quickly and are difficult to cope with in such large numbers with so few men who are accustomed to horse management. The few civilian wagons and carts available are being made use of to the best advantage but in most instances the harness is incomplete and in many cases rotten.

BILLETING. More stringent rules as to air space are being made and billeting areas are being increased in size in conformity to these rules. The advantage to the health of men will be great.

W. Wright Bemrose
Colonel
Comdg. 2/1 Sher: In: Inf: Bde

Confidential

War Diary

of

Headquarters 2/1 Sherwood Foresters Infantry Brigade

from 1 – 30 April 1915

Volume III

CONFIDENTIAL.

Instructions regarding War Diaries and Intelligence Summaries are contained in F.S. Regs., Part II. and the Staff Manual respectively. Title pages will be prepared in manuscript.

WAR DIARY
or
INTELLIGENCE SUMMARY.
(Erase heading not required.)

Army Form C. 2118.

HEADQUARTERS.
2/1 SHERWOOD FORESTERS INFANTRY BRIGADE.

Hour, Date, Place	Summary of Events and Information	Remarks and references to Appendices
LUTON. 1915. April.		
16.	2 Officers proceeded to join the Expeditionary Force during the month.	ad
	20 Officers 248 N.C.O's and Men of 2/7th Sherwood Foresters proceeded to BROXBOURNE - BUMBLE GREEN - EPPING - NORTH WEALD BASSETT - GREEN STEAD GREEN - CHIPPING ONGAR and KELVEDON HATCH on Officers Road Piquet duty.	ad
17.	A further detachment proceeded to the same line.	ad
18.	The whole party returned to quarters.	ad
	100 men in each Battalion were transferred (on paper) to 3rd. Line and remained with 2nd Line for training during the month.	ad
	Some Officers were lent to 3rd. Line to assist the training.	ad

Wright Reavoes
Colonel Cmdg.

2/1 Sherwood Foresters by bm

CONFIDENTIAL.   HEADQUARTERS.
                                 2/1 SHERWOOD FORESTER INFANTRY BRIGADE.

           STATEMENT TO ACCOMPANY WAR DIARY
                        for
                     APRIL. 1915.

TRAINING.   Physical Drill, Platoon and Company Drill, extended order
               drill, elementary musketry and night work and outposts
               by Companies with 1 hour Battalion drill weekly formed the
               chief items of training for this month.   Musketry on
               the open Range G.M.C.) was continued.   Bayonet Fighting
               was also carried out daily.   Some Field works made by the
               R.E. at Round Green were inspected and explained to all
               Battalions with much benefit.   March discipline was more
               strictly enforced when Battalions were marching to and from
               training grounds.
               The Stretcher Bearers of each Unit were brigaded one day a
               week and were instructed by Capt. W. Duncan, R.A.M.C. in
               their drill and duties.

DISCIPLINE.   The general behaviour of troops remains good, there being
               no serious crime during the month.   It has been
               impressed on O.C. Units that really good discipline and
               smartness both on and off parade can only be speedily
               ensured by the continual supervision of Company and Junior
               Officers.   These latter are inclined to let this be done
               by senior and Staff Officers.   The discipline of the
               Transport personnel is poor and efforts are being made to
               bring about a rapid improvement.

ADMINISTRATIVE SERVICES.

MEDICAL. All Units in the Brigade suffered to some extent from pediculi in Billets but otherwise the health of the Battalions was good. A great number of "Light Duty" men and men "excused duty" are to be seen about the streets and difficulty is being experienced in getting rid of these. Their presence is detrimental to the general state of the Brigade.

TRANSPORT. All Units had about 50 horses issued to them during the month. The horses were a very mixed lot, many being only partially trained. They were also in very poor condition.

ORDNANCE. All D.P. Rifles sent to 3rd Line also all C.L. M.L.E. Rifles except 120 per Unit which are to be retained for training purposes. Each Unit returned 200 M.L.E. Rifles to Weedon when they received Japanese Rifles, retaining only sufficient for training of 1st Foreign Draft Companies as above. The order to return these rifles to Weedon came separately and direct to Units and was acted upon before the order referring to return of Rifles to 3rd. Line.

EQUIPMENT. The Derbyshire Battalions, who were issued with 1914 Equipment had to send it back to the makers to be strengthened by having studs put through the back of the pack and the leather braces. This equipment has not been satisfactory at any time in its original form.

W. Wright Penrose,
Colonel Comdg.

Confidential

War Diary & Statement

of

Headquarters

2/1 Notts & Derby Inf: Bde

from 1st to 31st May 1915

Volume IV

CONFIDENTIAL. Army Form C. 2118.

WAR DIARY
or
INTELLIGENCE SUMMARY

(Erase heading not required.)

HEADQUARTERS.
2/1st NOTTS & DERBY INFANTRY BRIGADE.

Instructions regarding War Diaries and Intelligence Summaries are contained in F.S. Regs., Part II. and the Staff Manual respectively. Title Pages will be prepared in manuscript.

Place	Date	Hour	Summary of Events and Information	Remarks and references to Appendices
LUTON.	1915. May			
			3 Officers joined the Brigade during the month.	A.
			3 Officers proceeded overseas to join first Line Units with British Expeditionary Force.	A.
	7.		Orders received to separate Imperial Service men from Home Service men.	A.

Wright Reeves
Colonel
Comg. 2/1 Notts & Derby Inf. Bde.

CONFIDENTIAL.

HEADQUARTERS.
2/1st. NOTTS & DERBY
INFANTRY BRIGADE.

STATEMENT to accompany War Diary for

May 1915.

TRAINING. Ordinary training was practically put on one side during the month as Musketry Courses on the open Range were resumed and all Officers and N.C.O's were required for instructional purposes and Range Duties. In order to avoid waste of time on the Ranges Musketry was carried out by 2 parties daily. Those men who had started the Recruits Course in Musketry Regulations (Table A, Parts I & II, App IV.) completed that course and subsequently fired (Table B Part II App IV M.R.). Those who had not started the old course, started the General Musketry Course.
A special class for Young Officers under a Senior Officer was started on early morning parades.

ADMINISTRATIVE SERVICES.

MEDICAL. A special parade of sick in the Brigade disclosed the fact that there were 224. Of these 56 were marked as permanently unfit and had signed on for Imperial Service – 38 were Home Service men and were permanently unfit – Many of the remainder had not paraded for duty for weeks. Their presence with the Brigade is most undesirable but great difficulty is being experienced in getting rid of them. The Medical Examination on enlistment must be at fault. Apart from these men the general health of the Brigade is good.
Inoculation was started during the month and carried out in such a way that Musketry was not interfered with.

W. Wright Bemrose
Colonel
Comdg. 2/1 Notts & Derby Inf Bde

Confidential

War Diary & Statement

of

Headquarters 2/1 Notts & Derby Inf. Bde

from 1st to 30th June 1915

Volume V

CONFIDENTIAL.   Army Form C. 2118.

WAR DIARY
or
INTELLIGENCE SUMMARY

HEADQUARTERS. 2/1st NOTTS & DERBY INFANTRY BRIGADE.

(Erase heading not required.)

Instructions regarding War Diaries and Intelligence Summaries are contained in F. S. Regs., Part II. and the Staff Manual respectively. Title Pages will be prepared in manuscript.

Place	Date	Hour	Summary of Events and Information	Remarks and references to Appendices
LUTON.	1915 June 4.		Working parties of 2 Officers, 10 N.C.O's and 100 men per Battalion proceeded to Dunstable to prepare Camp.	ad
DUNSTABLE.	7.		The Imperial Service Officers, N.C.O's and men of the Brigade with a few Home Service men as additional Instructors moved to Dunstable :-	ad
			Brigade Headquarters. Officers - 4. Other Ranks - 10.	
			2/5th Battalion. " 12. " 497.	
			2/6th Battalion. " 24. " 834.	
			2/7th Battalion. " 32. " 957.	
			2/8th Battalion. " 18. " 1026.	
	17.		2 Officers proceeded to join the Overseas Brigade.	ad
	27.		730 Other ranks proceeded overseas to reinforce the 1st. Brigade.	ad
			4 Officers joined the Brigade all from 1st Line Units.	ad
			2 Chaplains joined the Brigade vice 2 sent overseas.	ad
			During the month a number of men were taken for Munition Works.	ad

Wright Reeves
Col.
Comdg. 2/1 Notts & Derby Inf. Bde.

CONFIDENTIAL.   HEADQUARTERS.
                                             2/1st NOTTS & DERBY
                                                     INFANTRY BRIGADE.

STATEMENT to accompany WAR DIARY
for June, 1915.

TRAINING.   Physical Training, Platoon and Company Drill, Musketry on
                 Miniature and open Range, Field Firing, Bayonet Fighting
                 and entrenching and night work were systematically carried
                 out.   Night work chiefly consisted of Outposts and
                 Night digging.   Cooking in Mess Tins was also practised.
                 Each Battalion spent one night in Bivouac, moving as a
                 complete Unit.

DISCIPLINE.   The general behaviour of troops improved very noticeably
                 after the Brigade went under canvas.

ADMINISTRATIVE SERVICES.

MEDICAL.   The health of the men is excellent.   The draft for
                 overseas could not have been more fit.   Later in the
                 month Scabies made its appearance.   Suitable arrangements
                 were made for bathing.

TRANSPORT.   The move from Luton was carried out with difficulty owing
                 to the Transport being entirely of civilian pattern and
                 the harness being rotten.

ORDNANCE.   The tentage supplied was of very poor quality and
                 insufficient for the number of men to be accommodated
                 until the draft left the Brigade.
                 The crowding in inadequate tent accommodation caused an
                 outbreak of Scabies.

                                        Wright Bemrose
                                              Colonel

                                        Comdg 2/1 Notts & Derby Inf Bde

Confidential

War Diary & Statement

of

Headquarters
2/1 Cheshire Bde Inf: Bde.

from 1st to 31st July 1915

Vol. VI

CONFIDENTIAL. Army Form C. 2118.

WAR DIARY
or
INTELLIGENCE SUMMARY

HEADQUARTERS. 2/1st. SHERWOOD FORESTER INFANTRY BRIGADE.

(Erase heading not required.)

Place	Date	Hour	Summary of Events and Information	Remarks and references to Appendices
DUNSTABLE.	1915. July 12.		Major P.M.Payne. T.D. took over command of 2/7th Battalion vice Lt.Col. G.A.Wigley (Med.unfit).	A
	13.		Major G.C.Aitchison took over command of 2/5th Battalion vice Lt.Col. M. Hunter (Home Service).	A
	14.		A draft of 60 N.C.O's and men arrived for the 2/6th Battalion from 3rd. Line.	A
	19.		Colonel E.W.S.K.Maconchy. C.B.,C.I.E.,D.S.O. assumed command of the Brigade vice Colonel W.Wright Bemrose. V.D. retired owing to Medical unfitness.	A
	20.		A Draft of 124 N.C.O's and men arrived for the 2/7th Battalion from 3rd. Line.	A
			A Draft of 180 N.C.O's and men arrived for the 2/8th Battalion from 3rd. Line.	A
	23.		2 Officers joined from 1st. Line temporarily pending resumption of duties overseas after sickness and wounds.	A
			24 Officers proceeded overseas as reinforcements to 1st. Line with British Expeditionary Force.	A

E.W.S.Maconchy
Colonel
Comdg 2/1 Sherwood Forester Infy Bde

CONFIDENTIAL.   HEADQUARTERS.
                                     2/1st. SHERWOOD FORESTER
                                              INFANTRY BRIGADE.

STATEMENT to accompany War Diary
for July, 1915.

TRAINING.   Training has proceeded satisfactorily on similar lines to those indicated for June with particular attention to Night digging and Night work generally.

ADMINISTRATIVE SERVICES.

MEDICAL.   Scabies has been on the increase during the month in spite of strenuous efforts made to erradicate the complaint.   Being unable to obtain from Ordnance any Marquees to be used as Isolation tents, a proportion of the Bell Tents of Units have been set aside for the purpose and further special arrangements for additional baths have been made and it is hoped that the evil will soon be stamped out.
Vaccination was started during the month and has proceeded satisfactorily.

TRANSPORT.   G.S. Limber Wagons are being issued to all Units by degrees.   The Horses quickly became accustomed to the new vehicles and special lessons in the fitting of harness are being given to all Transport men.

Confidential

War Diary & Statement

Of

Headquarters
178th Infantry Brigade

from 1st to 31st August 1915

Volume VII

CONFIDENTIAL.

Army Form C. 2118.

Instructions regarding War Diaries and Intelligence Summaries are contained in F.S. Regs., Part II. and the Staff Manual respectively. Title pages will be prepared in manuscript.

WAR DIARY
or
INTELLIGENCE SUMMARY.
(Erase heading not required.)

HEADQUARTERS.
2/1st SHERWOOD FORESTER INFANTRY BRIGADE.

Hour, Date, Place	Summary of Events and Information	Remarks and references to Appendices
DUNSTABLE. 1 – 11 August 1915.		
August 9th.	A part of the Brigade moved by road to WATFORD. 2/5 and 2/6th Battalions. 972.Officer & other ranks 2/1 N.M.Field Ambulance. 117.	Ap
	Recruits marched to AGNELLS FARM. 2/5th Battalion. Officers. Nil. Other ranks. 10. 2/6th " " 4 " " 105. 2/7th " " 4 " " 181. 2/8th " " 4 " " 227.	Ap
11th.	and completed the march to WATFORD on the 11th inst.	Ap
	Remainder of the Brigade marched by road to WATFORD. Brigade Headquarters. Officers. 3. Other ranks. 14. 2/7th Battalion. " 13. " " 446. 2/8th " " 19. " " 525. 2/1st N.M.Field Amb. " 2. " " 53.	Ap
WATFORD. HERTS. August 15.	264 N.C.O's and men proceeded to France as Drafts to 1st. Line. During the month 2 Officers joined from 3rd. Line and 17 Officers proceeded to France as reinforcements.	Ap

[signature] Colonel
Comdg. 2/1 Shu: I M[?] Bde

CONFIDENTIAL.
HEADQUARTERS.
2/1 SHERWOOD FORESTER
INFANTRY BRIGADE.

STATEMENT TO ACCOMPANY WAR DIARY
for AUGUST 1915.

TRAINING.
General Training has been carried out and more night work has been performed. All Units have been gradually trained in rapid advance from the prone position and considerable progress both in steadiness and speed are to be noticed. The marching capacity of the men is much improved and the long march to WATFORD was well carried out, the men looked very fit on their arrival. A class for young Officers has been formed in each Battalion with good results. Permission was obtained from Lord Ebury to dig permanent trenches in Moor Park. Ample Miniature Range accommodation was found in Watford.

ADMINISTRATIVE.
A good Camping ground was found in Cassiobury Park and all other arrangements were good.

TRANSPORT.
All Transport of material from Dunstable to Watford was carried out entirely by the Brigade Transport and the usual allotment of wagons from the A.S.C.

SANITATION.
A Camp Committee consisting of all 2nd in Command was made responsible for the cleanliness of the Camp Area. It was soon found that it was necessary to set aside one Bristol type wagon per Unit for the purpose of removing Horse Manure.
Hot Baths were arranged for the men at several works and in private houses.

MEDICAL.
A large amount of Dental work was completed throughout the Brigade during the month.

Confidential

WAR DIARY

of

Headquarters
178th Infantry Brigade

From 1st to 30th September 1915

Volume. VIII

CONFIDENTIAL.

Army Form C. 2118.

HEADQUARTERS.
178th. INFANTRY BRIGADE.

WAR DIARY
or
INTELLIGENCE SUMMARY.

(*Erase heading not required.*)

Instructions regarding War Diaries and Intelligence Summaries are contained in F.S. Regs., Part II. and the Staff Manual respectively. Title pages will be prepared in manuscript.

Hour, Date, Place	Summary of Events and Information	Remarks and references to Appendices
WATFORD. 1915.		
September 30th.	2 Officers proceeded overseas for active service.	do
	10 Officers joined on first appointment.	do
	6 Officers were attached from Highland Regiments.	do

W.G.Montgomery Colonel
Comdg 178° Infantry Brigade

CONFIDENTIAL.   178th. INFANTRY BRIGADE.
                                                          WATFORD.

                   STATEMENT to accompany War Diary
                            September 1915.

TRAINING.   During this month the chief items of training were trench
                  digging by day and night, Final assault on the Bayonet
                  Fighting Course by day and night, Rapid advances, siting
                  and laying out of trenches by night, Miniature Range
                  practice (grouping and application) every man once a
                  week, Bombing, Ammunition supply in the open and in
                  trenches and some close order drill.
                  Considerable progress has been made in all the above.
                  Brigade and Divisional Field Operations have also been
                  carried out and all ranks have shewn the greatest keenness
                  on each occasion.

DISCIPLINE.   Discipline has been stiffened up further during this
                  month and the behaviour of the men remains good.

ADMINISTRATIVE SERVICES.

MEDICAL.   Scabies has been bad during the month but has been
                  lessened by a new bathing order and by the fact that
                  each Unit now has a Medical Officer attached to it and
                  supervision is more thorough.
                  The majority of the men in the Brigade has been
                  vaccinated during the month - a few men suffered from
                  the after effects but generally speaking there was very
                  little trouble in this respect. No men were allowed
                  to leave the station but were kept under observation after
                  vaccination.
                  The shallow trench latrines have proved a great success

and it is considered to be the most satisfactory.

It has been found after many experiments that sullage water is most easily got rid of by means of shallow trenches in herring-bone patterns.

Large numbers of men have undergone Dental treatment.

SUPPLY. The quality of rations and forage remained good.

TRANSPORT. All Units have had 4 Field Kitchens issued during the month. It was at first though that light draught horses were not strong enough to draw the Field Kitchens but the disadvantage of the slow moving Heavy Draught Horse is great as a Column's pace is reduced and it has been now found that Light Draught Horses are all that is required.

Some Units have also received pack saddlery for the use of Company Pack Cobs. It would be a great advantage if detailed instructions were issued to Units with every set of pack saddlery showing how to fit, load and adjust such saddlery.

The whole of the Transport has been practiced in loading and unloading wagons at the L & N W Railway Sidings.

ORDNANCE. Tent Bottoms were issued late in the month. They were much needed.

BARRACK SERVICES. Barrack services were efficient.

[signature] Colonel

Comdg 178: Infantry Brigade

Confidential

War Diary & Statement

of

Headquarters
178th Infantry Brigade

from 1st to 31st October 1915

Volume IX

CONFIDENTIAL.

Army Form C. 2118.

Instructions regarding War Diaries and Intelligence
Summaries are contained in F.S. Regs., Part II.
and the Staff Manual respectively. Title pages
will be prepared in manuscript.

WAR DIARY
or
INTELLIGENCE SUMMARY.
(Erase heading not required.)

178th INFANTRY BRIGADE.
WATFORD.

Hour, Date, Place	Summary of Events and Information	Remarks and references to Appendices
WATFORD. Cassiobury Park Camp. 1 October 1915.	The Brigade was inspected by General Sir Leslie Rundle, G.C.B., G.C.M.G., &c. &c. in Gorhambury Park, St. Albans.	AA
13 " "	A Zeppelin passed over the Park adjoining the Camp at 9-25 p.m. proceeding in a Westerly direction, turned S and S.W. immediately after passing over the Camp and disappeared. The only warning received was that the lights of the Town were extinguished at the main. The Brigade turned out to their prearranged stations and remained out until recalled at 11-30 p.m.	AA
WATFORD TOWN. 18 " "	The Brigade moved into Billets in Watford Town from Camp - finding their own Transport with a little assistance from No. 4 Company, 59th. (North Midland) Divisional Train.	AA
19 " "	The Camping Ground was cleared up and left clean, all trenches being carefully filled in and all stumps levelled and hedges and fences made good.	AA
	On taking up quarters in Billets the Meat Ration was reduced from 1 lb. to 12 oz. per man.	AA
	During the month 16 Combatant Officers and one Army Chaplain proceeded overseas to join the Expeditionary Force in France.	AA

[signature] Colonel
Comdg. 178. Infantry Brigade

CONFIDENTIAL.

178th. INFANTRY BRIGADE.
WATFORD.

Statement to accompany War Diary for October. 1915.

TRAINING.

Battalion and Brigade training was carried out during the month of October and the Brigade took part in one Divisional Field Day. Every man in the Brigade was put through grouping and application practices in Musketry on the various Miniature Ranges once weekly. The results were good and although men benefit considerably from this type of Musketry it is found that the results are no criterion as to their efficiency with the full charge cartridge. Physical training has been carried out daily as have also Bayonet Fighting and practices over the Final Assault Course. An Officer who has had Bombing experience with the Expeditionary Force and is in civil life a mining Engineer and accustomed to the handling and use of explosives has been appointed Brigade Bombing Officer and good progress was made throughout the month both in Bombing and Trench warfare generally. This department of training would be better served if more opportunities of sending Officers to Courses on Bombing were afforded. The digging capacity of the Brigade is excellent, most of the men being recruited in Mining districts. They are rapidly improving in the matter of digging-in quickly and have a much improved knowledge of the various types of trenches now being used on service. Night work shows considerable improvement but there is much to be learnt in this respect still. Training has suffered through shortage of Officers owing to the constant drain of Officers for overseas service. Some Wood fighting has been practiced.

DISCIPLINE.

The good behaviour of the men is worthy of comment. The chief weakness is with the N.C.O's. They do not seem yet to realise their responsibility and there have been several cases of insubordinate behaviour to N.C.O's. Failure in this respect can also be traced to the short time during which the majority of N.C.O's in the Brigade have held their rank owing to drafts being called for. The discipline of the Brigade was not seriously affected by the move from Camp into Billets. Generally speaking the punishments awarded by C.O's have in the past been too mild ~~but a great~~ but a great improvement is now observed and in consequence minor offences are on the decrease.

ADMINISTRATION.

1. Medical.

Two of the Battalions have been without a Medical Officer until this month. This is a great detriment and the appointment of Medical Officers to these Battalions has proved of great benefit to them.

The Sanitary services are on the whole good. There are still some permanently unfit men in the Brigade and some who are obviously only half-witted. It would be of benefit if such men could be got rid of.

2. Supply service.

The quality of rations has been good, practically no complaints having been made.

3. Transport services.

The horses appear to have had too much work during the month and to have suffered somewhat during the first two weeks owing to cold and wet weather while picketed out. Where L.D. horses have to do the work of H.D. Horses, it would be better if they could be foraged as H.D. Horses.

4. Ordnance services.

75 Japanese rifles and 22,500 rounds of Japanese ammunition were withdrawn from each Battalion during the month and were sent to the 29th Provisional Battalion - leaving 525 rifles only per Battalion in charge.

BILLETING.

The move from Camp into Billets was carried out Regimentally on the 18th October. Billeting arrangements had previously been made under the general management of Major C. H. Heathcote, 2/6th Battalion, who carried out his duties in a most efficient manner. Large Halls were utilised at once for Central Messing and also for Billeting as far as could be arranged. Later in the month large Halls and Schools were used almost entirely for both purposes. A difficulty presented itself in the matter of heating these Halls, the fuel allowance based on cubic capacity with a maximum height of 10 feet from the floor being inadequate for heating in cold weather. The question is still under consideration but it is hoped that a new system may be instituted whereby the amount of fuel necessary for the proper heating may be arrived at and an allowance, in accordance with the necessity, made. Ventilation was also a difficulty it being found that the windows or other means of ventilation were generally too high to ensure good passage of air at all times. The above are the two chief drawbacks to central billeting but steps are being taken to remedy the latter.

HOSTILE AIR RAIDS.

Detailed arrangements (copies attached) have been made for the movements of all Units when accommodated in Billets upon warning being given of the approach of hostile aircraft and tests prove that the arrangements are understood.   Orders have been received that Zeppelins are to be fired at with rifle fire.

CAMP.

During the first 18 days of the month the Brigade remained under canvas, moving into Billets in the Town on the 18th. October.

The cleanliness of the whole Camp was very materially assisted owing to the fact that a road-way through the Camp with clinker cinders locally procured was made immediately troops occupied the ground.

[Signed] Colonel
Commg 178th Infantry Brigade
Watford

Subject. Hostile Aircraft

178. Infantry Bde.
Watford.

ORDERS ISSUED TO TROOPS UNDER MY COMMAND DURING THE
CAMPING SEASON.

It is notified for information that the following course will be adopted on warning being given that hostile airships are in the vicinity of the Camp.

The senior N.C.O. or man of each tent will immediately march the men of his tent by the nearest route in single file to a part of the ground allotted to his Battalion.

The 2/5th Battalion will be lined out close to the hedge between the Camp area and the RICKMANSWORTH Road, from the School boundary to the S entrance of the Camp.

2/6th Battalion from the S entrance to the Camp to a point half way along the Western boundary of the Camp under the trees.

2/7th Battalion from a point half way along the Western boundary of the Camp to the N.W. corner of the Camp area under the trees.

½ 2/8th Battalion along the fence between the Camp and Cassiobury Public Park.

½ 2/8th Battalion inside the park under the trees in Cassiobury Public Park.

In no case will men be bunched together. In every case protection from view must be found as far as possible.

In the event of a flare being dropped every man who is not already under cover will immediately lie down and remain absolutely still until the flare is burnt out.

The Fire Picquet for the day will also act in accordance with these instructions, but will take cover outside the Camp in a place best situated for immediate action if required.

178" Infantry Bde
Watford

(2)

O.C.Battalions will report in writing the situation chosen for their Fire Piquet.

Brigade Headquarters will move under the trees in Cassiobury Public Park near the main entrance to the Camp.

Reports to be sent to the small gate leading into the Public Park near the Y.M.C.A.Tent.

Perfect order and complete silence will be maintained and all lights will be extinguished before leaving the Camp.

Flash lights will not be used.

All ranks are to be specially warned that in no event are they to look skywards as the light colour of faces is known to be very easily distinguished from above.

Officers and N.C.O's will distribute themselves amongst the men of their Battalions and will take command of the parties near them.

Further suggestions are invited.

These arrangements are not to be spoken of or discussed outside the Camp or with any civilian.

Subject: Hostile Aircraft

178th Infantry Bde
Watford

A RÉSUMÉ OF ORDERS ISSUED TO TROOPS UNDER MY COMMAND, WHILST IN BILLETS.

In this Brigade each Battalion has detailed nightly 1 Officer and 50 other Ranks as a firing party - The Officer must be a Company Commander.

Each Battalion has had an open space on the outskirts of the Town of Watford allotted to it.

Ammunition is kept in each quarter guard at the rate of 50 rounds per man - This is taken in ready-made-up packets of 50, in ammunition boxes sealed to the various rendezvous and there issued as each party comes up.

Firing parties proceed to their respective rendezvous in small parties each under the command of the senior N.C.O. or man of each billet.

Only men who have fired a .303 or Japanese course are included in these firing parties.

No firing will take place except by the command of the Officer Commanding each party and then only if the Hostile Aircraft is showing an obvious intention of bombing, is flying at a low altitude and there is a reasonable chance of scoring hits.

Detailed arrangements have been made Regimentally for carrying out all the above plans.

Confidential

War Diary & Statement

of

Headquarters
    178th Inf: Div:

from 1st to 30th November 1915

Volume X.

Army Form C. 2118.

WAR DIARY
or
INTELLIGENCE SUMMARY.
(Erase heading not required.)

Instructions regarding War Diaries and Intelligence Summaries are contained in F.S. Regs., Part II. and the Staff Manual respectively. Title pages will be prepared in manuscript.

17th Infantry Bde.

Hour, Date, Place	Summary of Events and Information	Remarks and references to Appendices
WATFORD. November 1. 1915.	Musketry ordered but put off for rain.	
2.	Rehearsal of Bomb throwing – night digging – practice of Zeppelin raid arrangements.	
3.	Field Day, many casualties amongst Officers and N.C.O.'s – men drawn from ranks to accompany Stretcher bearers for instructional purposes.	
4.	Bombing display – Its chief uses (1) To accustom Bombers to handling explosives. (2) To accustom men to the sound of explosives. (3) To accustom men to the sight of flying earth. (4) To accustom men to getting in and out of trenches & passing orders. (5) To accustom horses to explosives.	
	Test of communications by night between Brigade Headquarters and Orderly Rooms. (2 hours first to last).	
	Training of all ranks in elementary First Aid, Stretcher carrying and French lessons.	
5.	Route marches, pay, &c. Interview with O.C. Local Volunteers Re Munitions Factory Guarding.	
6.	Usual Saturday work.	
7.	Zeppelin Raid Alarm.	

Army Form C. 2118.

WAR DIARY
or
INTELLIGENCE SUMMARY.
(Erase heading not required.)

Instructions regarding War Diaries and Intelligence Summaries are contained in F.S. Regs., Part II. and the Staff Manual respectively. Title pages will be prepared in manuscript.

Hour, Date, Place	Summary of Events and Information	Remarks and references to Appendices
WATFORD. November 8. 1915.	Repairing trenches in Moor Park after Bombing display.	Cd
9.	Field Operations, crossing bridges - carried out successfully - very wet.	Cd
10.	Inspection by Major-General Dickson (Inspector of Infantry). 2/5 and 2/8th Battalions - Callowland. a.m. revetting in the p.m. 2/6 and 2/7th Battalions - Moor Park. p.m. revetting in the a.m.	Cd
11.	654 men of the Brigade fired 2 practices of the Japanese Courses This leaves 42 men in each Battalion who have not yet fired a Course of any sort.	Cd
12.	Pouring rain all day. Battalions all under C.O's for interior economy. 37 G.S. Wagons arrived from Aymesbury.	Cd
13.	Battalion Route Marches. Report of General Manager of Munition Works - guard doubled in consequence - Posted by brigade major.	Cd
15.	All battalions in Moor Park on specialist work.	Cd
16.	Brigade inspected by Major-General R.N.R. Reade. C.B.	Cd
17.	18 mile route march. Notice to return all fit 1st Line officers to 3rd. Line and minimum number of officers fixed at brigade headquarters 4 - Machine Gun officer 1 - Transport officer 1 - Signalling officer 1 - majors and Captains 6 - subalterns 10.	Cd
18.	Night digging 6 hours. 2/5th. Battalion excellent.	Cd
" 19.	O.C. Battalions. Rifle check.	Cd

Army Form C. 2118.

WAR DIARY
or
INTELLIGENCE SUMMARY.
(Erase heading not required.)

Instructions regarding War Diaries and Intelligence Summaries are contained in F.S. Regs., Part II. and the Staff Manual respectively. Title pages will be prepared in manuscript.

Hour, Date, Place	Summary of Events and Information	Remarks and references to Appendices
WATFORD.		
November 20. 1915.	Route marches. 2/8th.Battalion scheme of altering routes worked very well.	aa
22.	All Battalions checking and packing Japanese Rifles and cleaning out .303 Rifles. Japanese ammunition sent away and .303 taken on charge of Units from 2/8th. battalion. Inspection of R.A.M.C. - 2-30. G.O.C. round digging (night) 2/6th & 2/7th Bns. started digging 6-15 ended 11-15.	aa aa aa aa
23.	G.O.C. witnessed bombing practice on Moor Park. Brigadier attends a Conference at St. Albans.	aa
24.	Visited Bedford Training Camp.	aa
25.	Divisional Route march.	aa
26.	Meeting of C.O's - Brigadier met all Company Commanders and platoon Commanders and explained new scheme for Company Training.	aa
27.	Battalion Route marches.	aa
29.	Special Company Training started - weather very bad - Went round all Miniature Ranges with Major Wykes. Divisional Musketry Officer.	aa
30.	Company Training is showing improvements all round already.	aa

CONFIDENTIAL.

178th. INFANTRY BRIGADE.

Statement to accompany War Diary for November 1915.

TRAINING.   Battalion, Brigade and Divisional Training was continued and on each day on which training was carried out in the Field a man from the ranks was attached to each trained stretcher bearer for elementary instruction in the methods of dealing with wounded and carrying stretchers.

First Aid Lectures were given to all ranks also. A pamphlet issued free by Major Maclure (London Scottish) has been distributed throughout the Brigade and should prove very useful in assisting the teaching of how to stop arterial bleeding and other elementary medical and surgical matters.

A large amount of revetting of various kinds was done on the Bayonet Fighting Courses and in the trenches at Moor Park, the materials being obtained from the woods in Cassiobury Park by permission of the Earl of Essex. The marching capacity of the Brigade is much improved since Camping grounds have been left. Where troops are under canvas and much of the training is being carried out on grass and in stubble fields more route marching should be done on hard roads.

MUSKETRY.   The miniature practices have been carried out regularly and to advantage. A short course (2 practices) was fired by about 650 men of the Brigade at Chalk Hill Range, St. Albans. The Range discipline was excellent but the instructors at the firing point were lacking in powers of imparting their instructions usefully and the Officers had a very poor knowledge of Range duties.

Night digging was performed by all Battalions. The 2/5th Battalion digging was excellent.

COMPANY TRAINING.
The G.O.C. instituted a system of special Company Training for 2 Companies in each Battalion for three consecutive weeks starting on the 29th November. All duty men, servants, grooms, cooks, &c. to be included in the training of these Companies. It is confidently expected that the results will be very good.

DISCIPLINE.
The good behaviour of the men is still maintained and the commission of more serious offences is on the decline. C.O's are at last beginning to adequately punish minor offences.

Discipline on the march is improving but C.O's and Adjutants do not check breaches of discipline so frequently as they might. The Transport still offend by not keeping to the left side of the road and pack pony leaders still have to be reminded that during halts their horses heads must be facing the right side of the road.

ADMINISTRATIVE.

MEDICAL.
Medical Boards have now rid the Brigade of many very undesirable men who have hitherto been on the strength for months and have attended no parades. Their presence with the Battalions has had a very bad effect.

The health of the Brigade has been generally good in spite of the very variable and rather severe weather.

SUPPLY SERVICES.	The quality of rations and forage remains good - waste has been considerably reduced but there is still room for improvement in this respect. The fault <u>must</u> be with Company Officers. If Company Officers exercised more careful supervision in their Company Cookhouses and paid more attention to the messing generally, less waste would occur.
TRANSPORT.	The Transport horses have looked better since going into Billets. A few cases of ringworm have occurred. 36 G.S. Limber Wagons were taken away from the Brigade for the immediate use of some Unit proceeding overseas and 37 G.S. Mark $\overline{X}$ Wagons were issued in their place during the month. It is understood that this is only a temporary arrangement and that Limber Wagons will again be issued shortly.
ORDNANCE.	Japanese Rifles were sent away on the 22nd November, 1915, L.E. & L.M. Rifles .305 being issued temporarily in their place. These latter rifles appeared to be in a very bad state but on being cleaned up and overhauled their condition was found to be not so bad as it at first appeared.
BARRACK SERVICES.	Great difficulty has been experienced in obtaining certain Barrack stores and even at the end of the month some Units were still without plates and mugs and benches and tables.
BILLETING.	Nearly all Units are now in Central Billets and Central Messes.
GENERAL.	All Bands were broken up and sent either away or back into the ranks.

4.

The number of Officers who are to serve with this Line was fixed at 23. This fixed number was not definitely stated to be a minimum or a maximum.

During the month the following N.C.O's and men have left the Brigade for the reasons stated :-

To Provisional Battalion.	196
To 3rd. Line.	4
To other Units.	14
Struck off as Medically unfit or deserters.	18
Granted Commissions.	3
	235.

Watford.

Capt.
Brigade Major.
178th. Infantry Brigade.

Confidential

War Diary & Statement of

Headquarters
178. Inf: Bde.

from 1st to 31st December 1915

VR: XI

CONFIDENTIAL.

Army Form C. 2118.

WAR DIARY
or
INTELLIGENCE SUMMARY.

178th. INFANTRY BRIGADE.

(Erase heading not required.)

Instructions regarding War Diaries and Intelligence Summaries are contained in F. S. Regs., Part II. and the Staff Manual respectively. Title pages will be prepared in manuscript.

Hour, Date, Place	Summary of Events and Information	Remarks and references to Appendices
WATFORD		
1 December 1915.	Brigade Route March cancelled after proceeding 2 miles owing to heavy rain. The march to the Starting Point was much improved but Divisional Train was badly marshalled at Starting Point.	AA
2 "	Lectures and Rifle cleaning carried out.	AA
3 "	G.O.C. visited area. Night operations of 2/5th Battalion - Special Companies.	AA
7 "	Pouring rain all day - Night operations cancelled.	AA
8 "	Brigadier and Staff Captain attended Divisional Headquarters - Conference on Divisional Scheme. Conference on Battalion Route marches under senior Captains. Administrative schemes.	AA
9 "	Very wet day - schemes of C.O's criticised - meeting for next days work.	AA
10 "	Wet day - training much interfered with.	AA
13 "	The results of 2 weeks Company Training were obviously excellent for both Officers and men.	AA
16-21 "	Inspection of Companies who had carried out Special Training by Brigadier.	AA
22 "	Christmas leave started - 10% of establishment going every 5 days.	AA

Army Form C. 2118.

WAR DIARY
or
INTELLIGENCE SUMMARY.
(Erase heading not required.)

Instructions regarding War Diaries and Intelligence Summaries are contained in F. S. Regs., Part II. and the Staff Manual respectively. Title pages will be prepared in manuscript.

Hour, Date, Place	Summary of Events and Information	Remarks and references to Appendices
23 - 31st December 1915.	Battalions under C.O's for General Training.	
28th. December 1915.	Colonel E.W.S.K. Maconchy. C.B.,C.I.E.,D.S.O. proceeded to France on a 4 days instructional tour.	

W.S.Maconchy/Colonel

Cmmdg. 178 Infantry Brigade.

CONFIDENTIAL.

178th. INFANTRY BRIGADE.
WATFORD.

STATEMENT TO ACCOMPANY WAR DIARY

for

December. 1915.

TRAINING.   The system of putting 2 Companies (complete with all details) into 3 weeks Company Training has been most beneficial throughout the Brigade.   Considerable difficulty has been experienced in every Battalion in replacing the Transport men by others with little or no experience with Horses drawn from the remainder of the Battalion but this difficulty was surmounted.   There would be no difficulties of this kind if Battalions were up to strength or even were 800 strong.   Another difficulty which has been less easily met is that caused by the shortage of Officers.   With Units <u>organised</u> on War Establishment basis but with the minimum limit of 23 Officers per Battalion and with many Officers away on Courses of Instruction the training by Officers has been much interfered with and good supervision is impossible. During training of special Companies, all other available Officers and all remaining Company Sergeant Majors have been given lectures and practical training in Bombing. No. 4 Company Divisional Train A.S.C. has been included in Brigade Route Marches during the month.   This is a very necessary addition to training, for without practice in marshalling of vehicles, and in making watering and feeding

(2).

arrangements the difficulties of arranging such details are apt to be overlooked. All Transport and Train Units have been practiced in harnessing, in-spanning and moving off in complete darkness without lamps or lights of any description. On all route marches a pick or a shovel is issued to every 4 men ~~and~~ to be carried in turn by each so that each carries equipment and a tool for about 5 miles. They are now quite efficient in carrying them noiselessly and with apparent ease.

DISCIPLINE. The capacity of Officers in the Brigade in writing orders is poor but is showing improvement. Great stress has been laid on the subject of "reading orders" carefully so that they may be accurately obeyed, and of Captains enforcing march discipline when senior Officers are not present.

MEDICAL. The general health of the Brigade is still good in spite of the inclement weather. There is a certain amount of scabies and lice among all Battalions and C.O's have been instructed to take measures to see that every man has a bath once a week. The Bathing facilities in this area are good.

TRANSPORT. There is a great improvement in the turn-out of all First Line Transport. Their march discipline is much improved. Their personal responsibility for the pack animals with their Companies has been impressed on all Company Officers.

Greasing of wheels and the general care of wagons has also been made a special point in Transport Training.

SUPPLY. Central Messing has been carried out in all Battalions under the supervision of Company Officers. A great improvement in messing arrangements is noticeable now that Officers are

(3).

taking a greater interest. The supply of Government Rations has been adequate and the quality good. Selected Officers from the Brigade attended a demonstration at the School of Cookery, London Colney and received great benefit.

ORDNANCE. Serviceable .303 Rifles and Machine Guns are much needed.

BARRACK SERVICES. Barrack Services were well carried out. The chief difficulty appears to be the shortage of material and supplies generally but where the Barrack Officer has the stores which were wanted he has supplied them as expeditiously as possible.

BILLETING. Central Billeting and Messing has been extended to practically the whole Brigade and is found to be very much better than the system of billeting in private houses and largely contributes to the maintenance of good health and good discipline.

[signature] Colonel

Comdg. 178th Infantry Brigade

Confidential

WAR DIARY

of

Headquarters

178th Infantry Brigade

From 1st to 31st January 1916.

VOLUME XII

CONFIDENTIAL.

178th INFANTRY BRIGADE.

Army Form C. 2118.

WAR DIARY
or
INTELLIGENCE SUMMARY.

(Erase heading not required.)

Instructions regarding War Diaries and Intelligence Summaries are contained in F. S. Regs., Part II. and the Staff Manual respectively. Title pages will be prepared in manuscript.

Hour, Date, Place	Summary of Events and Information	Remarks and references to Appendices
WATFORD. 1916.		
January 9.	1 Officer 3 N.C.O's and 12 men R.E. reported to teach Companies Field work.	ap
12.	2/1st N.M. Field Ambulance left this station and the 2/2nd. N.M. Field Ambulance took over their quarters in Watford.	ap
21.	Divisional Administrative Scheme.	ap
22 - 23.	140 Recruits (Lord Derbys) arrived in the Brigade during 2 days.	ap
28.	332 Derby Recruits have arrived up to this date. Zeppelins were reported at 8-35 p.m. Troops stood to their posts until 11-10 p.m. but no further action was necessary.	
29.	Total number of "Derby Group" recruits who have joined to this date is 361. the remaining 2 Companies in each Battalion completed Special Training to-day.	ap

Watford ?
20.7.16 S

W.B.Wroconchy Col.
Comdg 178th Inf. Bde.

CONFIDENTIAL.

178th. INFANTRY BRIGADE.
WATFORD.

STATEMENT TO ACCOMPANY WAR DIARY
for January 1916.

TRAINING. The remaining Companies of this Brigade carried out special Company Training during the month with, again, excellent results. Included in their training was special instruction by an R.E. Field Company Officer and 12 N.C.O's and men who took each Company in turn in Field work, entrenching, obstacle making, revetting &c. On route marches during the month, more men have fallen out. The reason is being enquired into.
A Divisional Administrative Scheme proved very instructive to all concerned. The Training of Machine Gun Sections is much hampered by the lack of guns.

DISCIPLINE. Remains good.

ADMINISTRATIVE. Medical. All recruits from "Derby Groups" are being inoculated immediately on their arrival.
Transport. Difficulty is being experienced in obtaining Lamps (side and rear) for Transport wagons and carts.
Supply. Contractors have been employed in accordance with orders for the supply of groceries &c. to Units. The system is not found to be entirely satisfactory especially as regards the prices at which the men obtain the Supplies when compared with local market rate. Another adverse result of employing Army Contractors is that the local tradesmen will not now purchase dripping from Units as heretofore.

[signature]
Colonel
Comdg. 178th Inf. Brigade

Confidential

War Diary

— of —

Headquarters 178 Infantry Bde

from 1st to 29th February 1916.

Vol: XIII

CONFIDENTIAL.

Army Form C. 2118.

WAR DIARY
or
INTELLIGENCE SUMMARY.
(Erase heading not required.)

HEADQUARTERS.
178th. INFANTRY BRIGADE.

Hour, Date, Place	Summary of Events and Information	Remarks and references to Appendices
WATFORD. 1916.		
February 3.	602 new Recruits have reported to the Brigade to this date.	QD
6.	100 Short Rifles were issued by Ordnance to each Battalion and were re-issued to Recruits for instructional purposes.	QD
	5 Piquets (Air Bandit, Observation Posts were posted at various points West of Watford.	QD
9.	Brigade Administrative Scheme.	QD
12.	2/8th Battalion completed numbers of recruits required – 327.	QD
13.	2/7th.Battalion " " " " – 338.	QD
14.	Major-General E.A.Sandbach C.B.,D.S.O. assumed command of the Division.	QD
15.	2/6th Battalion completed numbers of recruits required – 350.	QD
18.	50 Rifles sent to R.E. Radlett on loan. 2 Officers, 104 Other ranks sent to Headquarters, Dunmow on guard duty.	QD
20.	2/5th Battalion completed numbers of recruits required – 371.	QD
21.	Lt.Col. C. Fane D.S.O. reported for duty and assumed command of the 2/7th. Battalion from this date.	QD
24.	All leave cancelled and all Officers on leave were recalled.	QD
28.	O.C. 2/5th Battalion and The Brigade Major proceeded to France on an instructional Tour.	QD
29.	Practice Emergency Move. "Table B".	QD

CONFIDENTIAL. HEADQUARTERS.
178th. INFANTRY BRIGADE.
WATFORD.

STATEMENT to accompany War Diary for the month of
FEBRUARY. 1916.

TRAINING. Special Company Training was again instituted on somewhat different lines. 2 Companies per Battalion being struck off for training on four consecutive days, the remaining 2 Companies finding all duties and fatigues and Bombers to be found from Duty Companies only. Every effort was made to carry out the scheme but it was found to be impracticable in some departments of training owing chiefly to the small numbers of men available in each Battalion. A Brigade Administrative Scheme again proved of the greatest benefit both to R.A.M.C. Units and also to Gunners and Infantry. A sudden retirement ordered in the middle of operations was the means of teaching all Units many things. Bombers, Machine Gunners and Signallers progressed in their training and special attention was directed to the subject of use of ground in attack and defence. Each Battalion completed with Recruits up to a total strength of 850. The class of Recruit is excellent and the rapidity with which they are picking up the details of training is most marked. Very instructive Lectures on Asphyxiating Gasses and on Bayonet Fighting were delivered to the Brigade during the month.

DISCIPLINE. The Discipline remains good and the moral of the Brigade is high in spite of the very depressing weather conditions and the hard work.

ADMINISTRATIVE SERVICES.

MEDICAL. There has been a certain amount of Rheumatism and an average number of cases of infectious colds and catarrh especially towards the latter end of the month, quite a normal state of affairs at this time of the year. Inoculation and Vaccination of Recruits has been pushed forward. Inoculation is almost complete but vaccination has been delayed owing to the vaccene being improcurable.

SUPPLY. Normal.

TRANSPORT. All Civilian pattern vehicles and harness were sent to St. Albans during the month (including Bristol wagons). At least one such wagon is really needed by each unit to enable the carting of manure to be efficiently dealt with.

ORDNANCE. Each Battalion had 100 new short L.E.Rifles issued during the early part of the month.

BILLETING. The Billeting of large numbers of men in large buildings tends to the spreading of infectious colds so prevalent at this time of the year. Men suffering from such ailments also require warmer quarters and it would be a benefit if they might be removed to Billets temporarily until they recover normal health again.

Colonel
Comdg. 178 Infantry Brigade

Confidential

War Diary
of
Headquarters
178th Infantry Brigade

From 1st to 31st March 1916

Volume XIV

CONFIDENTIAL.　　　　　　　　　　Army Form C. 2118.

Instructions regarding War Diaries and Intelligence Summaries are contained in F. S. Regs., Part II. and the Staff Manual respectively. Title Pages will be prepared in manuscript.

WAR DIARY
or
INTELLIGENCE SUMMARY
(Erase heading not required.)

HEADQUARTERS.
178th. INFANTRY BRIGADE.

Place	Date	Hour	Summary of Events and Information	Remarks and references to Appendices
WATFORD.	1916. March 4.		12 Lewis Guns arrived.	A1
	5.		Hostile Aircraft reported at Grimsby, Cambridge and Dunmow – arrangements worked well.	A2
	7.		700 Short L.E. Rifles arrived each for the 2/5th and 2/6th Battalions.	A2
			The G.O.C. 3rd. Army inspected the Brigade recruits.	A2
	9.		Major General Dickson, Inspector of Infantry inspected the Brigade.	A2
	31.		Hostile Aircraft reported in the vicinity of Watford. Troops turned out but no aircraft observed or heard.	A2
			The Brigade was warned that it will proceed to a new training centre.	A2
			During the month 10 Officers reported for light duty with the Brigade – All have seen service in the Field during this War.	A2

W.J.McMahon
Comdg. 178 Infantry Brigade.
Colonel

CONFIDENTIAL.

HEADQUARTERS.
178th. INFANTRY BRIGADE.

STATEMENT to accompany War Diary for
March. 1916.

TRAINING.   Special attention has been given to Grenade training during the month and a marked improvement has been seen. Bomb throwing has been included in the training of recruits.
The organisation of Battalions in trenches and the attack from trenches was also practised.
The very wet weather materially affected all classes of training.

DISCIPLINE.   Remained good.

ORDNANCE.   Each Battalion had 700 new short L.E. Rifles issued, making a total on charge of 800 per Battalion. 4 Lewis Guns were also issued to each Battalion.
Mark VI Ammunition will not pass from the magazines of the short rifle into the lead, the reason being that the horns on the forward part of the magazine are slightly too close together and the last and last but one of the cartridges are liable to get caught and cause a jamb. This defect has been pointed out to higher authority.

[signature]
Colonel

Comdg. 178th Infantry Brigade

CONFIDENTIAL.

Army Form C. 2118.

Instructions regarding War Diaries and Intelligence Summaries are contained in F. S. Regs., Part II. and the Staff Manual respectively. Title pages will be prepared in manuscript.

WAR DIARY
or
INTELLIGENCE SUMMARY.

(Erase heading not required.)

HEADQUARTERS.
178th. INFANTRY BRIGADE.

May 16

Place	Date	Hour	Summary of Events and Information	Remarks and references to Appendices
ROYAL HOSPITAL. KILMAINHAM.	1916. May 1.		Situation of Troops in and attached to Brigade. Brigade Headquarters. Royal Hospital, KILMAINHAM. 5th Battalion Sherwood Foresters (less 5 Officers 209 men ARKLOW) KINGSBRIDGE STATION. 6th Battalion Sherwood Foresters. Royal Hospital, KILMAINHAM. 7th Battalion Sherwood Foresters. (less 1 Officer 27 men Prison duty RICHMOND BARRACKS) Royal Hospital, KILMAINHAM. 8th Battalion Sherwood Foresters. ATHENRY. (unofficially stated to be at LOUGHREA). No 2 Company Divisional Train. A.S.C. Royal Hospital, KILMAINHAM. No 2 Field Company. R.E. ditto. ditto. Nos. 2 and 5 Platoons Divisional Cyclist Co. ditto. ditto. Passes required by all persons to go through cordon line except women and except children and men under 14 and over 65 years of age. 6th Battalion arrived at KILMAINHAM Royal Hospital from street duty. 29 Officers 830 Other Ranks. Casualties (full) reported to have occurred to date :-	

	Killed.	Died of Wounds.	Wounded.	Missing.
OFFICERS.				
7th Battalion.	3	Nil.	8	Nil.
8th Battalion.	1	1	6	Nil.
OTHER RANKS.				
6th Battalion.	1	Nil.	5	Nil.
7th Battalion.	5	Nil.	66	67.
8th Battalion.	6	Nil.	49	16.

May 2.		Total casualties in other ranks reported to-day :-	

	Killed.	Died of Wounds.	Wounded.	Missing.
6th Battalion.	1	Nil.	5	Nil.
7th Battalion.	5	Nil.	66	63.
8th Battalion.	6	Nil.	49	16.
	12	Nil.	120	79

1 Company of 6th Bn. Sherwood Foresters under Major C. H. Heathcote sent to Richmond Barracks as additional guard for prisoners.
Free circulation of all persons without passes permitted within the outer cordon.
7th Battalion provided an escort of 500 men and Officers to escort prisoners from RICHMOND BARRACKS to NORTH WALL - 1 Officer and 20 men proceeded over to England (Stafford).

CONFIDENTIAL.   Army Form C. 2118.

Instructions regarding War Diaries and Intelligence
Summaries are contained in F. S. Regs., Part II.
and the Staff Manual respectively. Title pages
will be prepared in manuscript.

WAR DIARY
or
INTELLIGENCE SUMMARY.
(Erase heading not required.)

HEADQUARTERS.
178th. INFANTRY BRIGADE.

Place	Date	Hour	Summary of Events and Information	Remarks and references to Appendices
Royal Hospital. KILMAINHAM. DUBLIN.	May 3.		Casualties amended :- 7th. Battalion. Other ranks wounded 57 instead of 66 - Missing 30 instead of 63. 8th. Battalion. Other ranks wounded 52 instead of 49 - Missing 12 instead of 16. 27 men of 7th Battalion were relieved by 1 Platoon and 25 men of 6th Battalion in RICHMOND BARRACKS and proceeded to rejoin their Battalion at PORTOBELLO BARRACKS. 51 men of the 7th Battalion and 4 men of the 8th Battalion rejoined at KILMAINHAM Royal Hospital from BEGGARS BUSH BARRACKS where they had been detained by O.C. Barracks as an additional guard during the fighting of the 26th to 30th April and afterwards - considerable difficulty was experienced in persuading this officer to relieve these men even to-day. 5 Officers and 150 men moved from Royal Hospital KILMAINHAM to garrison ISLAND BRIDGE BARRACKS. The 5th and 7th Battalions took up cordon duty. No 2 Field Company, R.E. left Royal Hospital and proceeded to PHOENIX PARK to prepare a Divisional Camp. 2 armoured cars arrived from RICHMOND BARRACKS for use of the Brigade and were detailed to report, 1 to O.C. 5th Battalion KINGSBRIDGE STATION and the other to O.C. 7th. Battalion at PORTOBELLO BARRACKS. RATHMINES AND INCHICORE Tramway system resumed work, trams running every ¼ hour only and to be stopped for examination at PORTOBELLO BRIDGE and KILMAINHAM respectively. Disposition of Troops to-day.- Brigade Headquarters. KILMAINHAM Royal Hospital. 5th Bn. Sherwood Foresters. 1 Officer 20 Other ranks at Numbers 4, 7 & 9 Bridges over } River LIFFEY. } 1 Officer 20 Other ranks at each of - CITY HALL. N end of BACK LANE. S end of STEVENS LANE. 1 Officer 25 Other ranks at each of - Junction of ST JOHNS ROAD and CONYNGHAM ROAD. 1 Officer 17 Other ranks at each of - TUNNEL and THE RAILWAY BRIDGE. Remainder of Battalion as Garrison for KINGSBRIDGE STATION.	

CONFIDENTIAL.

Army Form C. 2118.

Instructions regarding War Diaries and Intelligence
Summaries are contained in F.S. Regs., Part II.
and the Staff Manual respectively. Title pages
will be prepared in manuscript.

HEADQUARTERS.
178th. INFANTRY BRIGADE.

WAR DIARY
or
INTELLIGENCE SUMMARY.
(*Erase heading not required.*)

Place	Date	Hour	Summary of Events and Information	Remarks and references to Appendices
Royal Hospital. KILMAINHAM. DUBLIN.	1916. May 3.		6th Bn. Sherwood Foresters. Headquarters, 1 Company & details at Royal Barracks, KILMAINHAM. 1 Company in ISLAND BRIDGE BARRACKS. 1 Company.) 1 Platoon.) RICHMOND BARRACKS. 25 men.) 7th.Bn. Sherwood Foresters. Headquarters, and 1 Company (90 men) at PORTOBELLO BARRACKS. 1 Company from Corners of CAMDEN ROW and MONTAGUE STREET to PORTOBELLO BRIDGE with Company Headquarters in Picture House CAMDEN ST. 1 Company PORTOBELLO BRIDGE (inclusive) to DOLPHINS BARN BRIDGE (exclusive). 1 Company DOLPHINS BARN BRIDGE (inclusive) To ROYAL HOSPITAL AVENUE. 8th Bn. Sherwood Foresters - at or in the neighbourhood of ATHLONE (No 3 Mobile Column). 2nd Field Ambulance.) No.2 Company 59th Divl. Train.A.S.C.) Royal Hospital KILMAINHAM. 2 Platoons 59th Divisional Cyclist Co left Royal Hospital and proceeded to ROYAL BARRACKS. Casualties amended :- Killed. Wounded. Missing. OTHER RANKS. 6th Bn.Sherwood Foresters. 1 5 Nil. 7th Bn.Sherwood Foresters. 14 63. 29. 8th Bn.Sherwood Foresters. 6 50 10. 50 men withdrawn from Island Bridge Barracks to accompany 6th Battalion on Detachment duty 6th Battalion Headquarters and 16 Officers.) 487 Other ranks.) Proceeded on detachment to LONGFORD under 26 Horses.) command of Lt.Col. H.S.Hodgkin. D.S.O. 9 wagons.) 7 Bicycles.)	
	4.		Lt. Col. H.S. HODGKIN and Capt & Adjt. V.H.E. LANGFORD ordered to return to give evidence against Sein Fein prisoners. They reported at 4-30 p.m. 2 Officers and 100 Other ranks from 7th Battalion sent from PORTOBELLO BARRACKS to reinforce guard at RICHMOND BARRACKS.	

CONFIDENTIAL.

Instructions regarding War Diaries and Intelligence Summaries are contained in F.S. Regs., Part II. and the Staff Manual respectively. Title pages will be prepared in manuscript.

Army Form C. 2118.

WAR DIARY
or
INTELLIGENCE SUMMARY.
(Erase heading not required.)

HEADQUARTERS.
178th. INFANTRY BRIGADE.

Place	Date	Hour	Summary of Events and Information	Remarks and references to Appendices

Royal Hospital. KILMAINHAM. DUBLIN.	1916. May 5.		Casualty list amended -
			
			                                  Killed. Wounded. Missing.
			OTHER RANKS. 6th Bn. Sherwood Foresters. 1 5 Nil.
			                  7th Bn. Sherwood Foresters. 15 63 17.
			                  8th Bn. Sherwood Foresters. 6 50 10.
			
			Field Post Office established at Royal Hospital KILMAINHAM - designation A.P.O: 42 : H.D. 5th Battalion moved Headquarters from KINGSBRIDGE STATION to 98 JAMES STREET. No passes required from to-day except through IRISHTOWN CORDON. N.C.O's and men allowed to walk out on pass before 7-30 p.m. within cordon only. All civilians to be in doors between 8-30 p.m. and 5-0 a.m.	

	6.		Orders issued to form an inner cordon :-
			                      (Along the Canal on the SOUTH.
			                      (RICHMOND STREET - LOWER CAMDEN STREET on the EAST.
			7th. Battalion. (CAMDEN ROW - LONG LANE on the NORTH.
			                      (LOWER and UPPER CLANBRASSIL STREET on the WEST.
			
			5th Battalion relieved by 6th Reserve Cavalry (400 men). Regiment
			An extension of the inner cordon sanctioned by Divisional Headquarters :-
			                      (WEXFORD STREET - REDMONDS HILL and PETER ROW on the EAST.
			6TH Reserve Regt Cavalry.(PETER STREET - CROSS KELVIN STREET and UPPER KELVIN STREET on the NORTH.
			                      (NEW STREET on the WEST.
			
			Casualties amended :-
			                                  Killed. Wounded. Missing.
			OTHER RANKS. 6th Bn. Sherwood Foresters. 5 1 Nil.
			                  7th Bn. Sherwood Foresters. 15 62 11.
			                  8th Bn. Sherwood Foresters. 6 50 10.
			
			5th Battalion reached Royal Hospital. Strength :-
			Officers. 19 - Other ranks 626. Horses & Mules 57 - Vehicles 13 - Field Kitchens 4 - Bicycles 8.	

CONFIDENTIAL.

Army Form C. 2118.

Instructions regarding War Diaries and Intelligence Summaries are contained in F. S. Regs., Part II. and the Staff Manual respectively. Title pages will be prepared in manuscript.

WAR DIARY
or
INTELLIGENCE SUMMARY.
(Erase heading not required.)

HEADQUARTERS.
178th. INFANTRY BRIGADE.

Place	Date	Hour	Summary of Events and Information	Remarks and references to Appendices
Royal Hospital KILMAINHAM. DUBLIN.	1916. May 7.		Casualty amendments :- OTHER RANKS. Killed. Wounded. Missing. 6th. Bn. Sherwood Foresters. 1 5 Nil. 7th. Bn. Sherwood Foresters. 15 63 7. 8th. Bn. Sherwood Foresters. 6 50 10. The inner cordon line south of River LIFFEY was established and house to house searches were instituted.	
	8.		Casualty amendments :- OTHER RANKS. Killed. Died of Wounds. Wounded. Missing. 6th. Bn. Sherwood Foresters. 1 Nil. 5 Nil. 7th. Bn. Sherwood Foresters. 14 1 68 3. 8th. Bn. Sherwood Foresters. 6 1 50 4. All tram circuits allowed to run except along HARRINGTON STREET (between RICHMOND STREET and CLANBRASSIL STREET) all trams to stop and be examined at examining posts. Movements of Troops. One Company 7th. Battalion from PORTOBELLO BARRACKS relieved another Company of the same Battalion at RICHMOND BARRACKS making an increase of 30 men. One Officer and 55 men of the 5th Battalion moved from Royal Hospital KILMAINHAM to RICHMOND BARRACKS to bring total on prison guard duty to 400 Other ranks. Disposition of troops to-day. Brigade Headquarters. complete - Royal Hospital KILMAINHAM. 6th Res. Cavalry Detachment. Headquarters (Major Collis) KINGSBRIDGE STATION. 140 men on inner cordon line. Remainder on picquet duty. 5th Bn Sherwood Foresters. Headquarters - Royal Hospital KILMAINHAM. (a) 18 Officers. 561 Other ranks. Horses and Mules. 57. Vehicles. 13. Field Kitchens. 4. Bicycles. 8. (b) On Detachment at ARKLOW. 5 Officers. (under Major R.B.Rickman). 209 Other ranks.	

CONFIDENTIAL.   Army Form C. 2118.

HEADQUARTERS.
178th. INFANTRY BRIGADE.

WAR DIARY
or
INTELLIGENCE SUMMARY.
(Erase heading not required.)

Place	Date	Hour	Summary of Events and Information	Remarks and references to Appendices

Royal Hospital. KILMAINHAM. DUBLIN.	1916. May. 8.		6th Bn. Sherwood Foresters. Headquarters. LONGFORD.
			                          Officers. 16.
			                          Other ranks. 487.
			                          Horses. 26.
			                          Vehicles. 9.
			                          Bicycles. 7.
			
			                          Officers. 5.)
			                          Other ranks. 117.) ISLAND BRIDGE BARRACKS.
			                          Field Kitchens. 1.)
			
			                          Officers. 7.)
			                          Other ranks. 179.) RICHMOND BARRACKS.
			                          Bicycles. 1.)
			
			7th Bn. Sherwood Foresters. Headquarters. PORTOBELLO BARRACKS.
			                less Officers. 5.)
			                          Other ranks. 157.)
			                          Kitchen. 1.) RICHMOND BARRACKS.
			                          Bicycles. 1.)
			
			8th Bn. Sherwood Foresters. Headquarters. ATHLONE.
			
			2nd Field Ambulance.) Royal Hospital KILMAINHAM.
			2 Company. Divl. Train. A.S.C.) Ditto.
			
			8 Officers 400 Other ranks went as escort to prisoners from RICHMOND BARRACKS to NORTH WALL. 4 Officers and 300 men returning to quarters on completion of duty. 4 Officers and 100 men proceeding to England.
			
			Preliminary orders received by Brigade from Headquarters Division that when the cordon is withdrawn accomodation must be found in public buildings, barracks &c. and that 3 guard posts will be required. Each of 2 Officers and 50 other ranks at KINGSBRIDGE STATION - ST PATRICKS PARK - and DOLPHINS BRIDGE. Officers & men to be billeted.	

	9.			

CONFIDENTIAL.

Army Form C. 2118.

WAR DIARY
or
INTELLIGENCE SUMMARY.

(Erase heading not required.)

HEADQUARTERS.
178th. INFANTRY BRIGADE.

Instructions regarding War Diaries and Intelligence Summaries are contained in F. S. Regs., Part II. and the Staff Manual respectively. Title pages will be prepared in manuscript.

Place	Date 1916.	Hour	Summary of Events and Information	Remarks and references to Appendices
Royal Hospital. KILMAINHAM, DUBLIN.	May. 9.		Telegram received from Major Goodman notifying his intention to report for duty as Brigade Major on the 10th. inst.	
	10.		1 Officer and 50 Other ranks reported back from England at 8 a.m. 1 Officer and 50 Other ranks reported back from England at 9-20 a.m. 16 men of 29th. Provisional Battalion arrived from England under Lieut. Whiston. 8 for 5th Battalion and 8 for 6th Battalion. The 6th Battalion men were sent to report to Major C.H.Heathcote at RICHMOND BARRACKS. Definite orders received that outer cordon will be withdrawn on Friday the 14th May. The inner cordon to remain on till further notice. Guards and Picquets to remain at Railway Stations and central places in the City to assist the Police if required.	
	11.		Major H.R.Goodman. Royal Irish Rifles arrived and assumed duty as Brigade Major.	
	12.		Connolly and MacDermott Rebel leaders shot at dawn. Close cordon withdrawn at 7 p.m. Heavy baggage arrived from England.	
	13.		" " " " "	
	14.		" " " " "	
	15. 16.		2/6th North Staffs attached to Brigade on departure of 176th Brigade to STRAFFAN. 2/5th Sherwood Foresters and 3 Officers 100 Other ranks 2/6th North Staffs moved to Camp on 15 acres PHOENIX PARK 13 Recruits from 24th Provisional Battalion arrived and were posted to 2/7th Sherwood Foresters. Pte. Charlesworth 2/8th Sherwood Foresters drowned while bathing in R. SHANNON at CARRICK ON SHANNON.	
	17.		" " " " " "	
	18.		" " " " " "	
	19.		" " " " " "	

CONFIDENTIAL.

Army Form C. 2118.

Instructions regarding War Diaries and Intelligence Summaries are contained in F.S. Regs., Part II. and the Staff Manual respectively. Title pages will be prepared in manuscript.

WAR DIARY or INTELLIGENCE SUMMARY.

HEADQUARTERS. 178th. INFANTRY BRIGADE.

(Erase heading not required.)

Place	Date	Hour	Summary of Events and Information	Remarks and references to Appendices
Royal Hospital. KILMAINHAM. DUBLIN.	1916. May. 20.		50 Recruits 2/7th Sherwood Foresters joined. 68 Recruits 2/8th Sherwood Foresters joined.	
	21.		- - - - - - - - -	
	22.		- - - - - - - - -	
	23.		83 Recruits 2/5th Sherwood Foresters joined.	
	24.		- - - - - - - - -	
	25.		Advance parties of 2 Officers and 50 Other ranks of 5th, 6th, & 8th Battalions left DUBLIN for CURRAGH CAMP.	
	26.		Advance parties of 3 Officers and 100 Other ranks of 7th. Battalion left DUBLIN for ORANMORE.	
	27.		Brigade Headquarters, Detachment 2/6th Sherwood Foresters, 182 men 2/5th Sherwood Foresters 68 Recruits 2/8th Sherwood Foresters No 4 Sec. 59th Divl Sig. Company 1 Section 3rd Field Ambulance (1st Column) proceeded from DUBLIN at 9 a.m. by route march to CURRAGH and billeted for night at RATHCOOLE. Half Battalion 2/6th and 2/8th Battalion arrived at CURRAGH by rail from LONGFORD and BALLINASLOE respectively.	
	28.		2/5th Sherwood Foresters Details, 2/8th Sherwood Foresters, No 4 Company A.S.C., 1 Section 3rd. Field Ambulance (Column 2) proceeded by route march from DUBLIN to CURRAGH and billeted at RATHCOOLE. Column 1 marched from RATHCOOLE to NAAS and billeted.	
	29.		Column 1 Marched from NAAS to CURRAGH and went into Camp and Hutments. Column 2 marched from RATHCOOLE to NAAS and billeted. Half Battalion 2/8th Sherwood Foresters arrived at CURRAGH by rail from ATHLONE.	
	30.		Column 2 marched from NAAS to CURRAGH and went into Camp and Hutments. 68 Recruits 2/8th Sherwood Foresters joined. 2/7th Battalion proceeded from DUBLIN to ORANMORE by rail and went into Camp.	
	31.		88 Recruits 2/7th Battalion joined.	

www.ingramcontent.com/pod-product-compliance
Lightning Source LLC
Chambersburg PA
CBHW081445160426
43193CB00013B/2396